DIANA
the
Radiant
PRINCESS

First published in Great Britain by Colour Library Books Ltd.
© 1983 Illustrations and text: Colour Library Books Ltd.,
   Guildford, Surrey, England.
This 1983 edition is published by Greenwich House, a division
of Arlington House, Inc. Distributed by Crown Publishers, Inc.
h g f e d c b a
Display and text filmsetting by Acesetters Ltd., Richmond, Surrey, England.
Printed and bound in Barcelona, Spain by JISA-RIEUSSET and EUROBINDER.
ISBN 0 517 437953

DIANA
the
Radiant
PRINCESS

GREENWICH HOUSE

DIANA THE RADIANT PRINCESS

One cold March evening in 1983 a Royal Australian Air Force plane took off from London bound for Australia. It was loaded with trunks of dresses, suits, coats, jackets and fashion accessories – and there are many who would have paid a small fortune to find out what the clothes looked like and who had designed them. For they had been cut, stitched, pressed and packed for the Princess of Wales' first-ever tour.

Fashion writers and reporters around the world had spent months trying to discover the details of the exclusive Royal wardrobe, for in the two years from her engagement to her first Royal tour the young Princess had swapped her informal Sloane Ranger fashions for formal but fetching styles fit for a working Royal. She had achieved her Royal goal with staggering speed and with very few mistakes, and there were two spin-offs from her achievement – she created some internationally popular fashions, and she made a name for herself as a fashion leader.

The fashion line she created as a Princess was a far cry from the clothes she wore in the months leading up to her engagement when she worked at the Young England kindergarten in Pimlico. But as she trundled pushchairs along the streets of London or took her charges out for walks, clothes were the last thing on Lady Diana's mind. Like any young lady in love she must have wanted to tell the world about her romance – but she couldn't for she had fallen in love with the heir to the British throne, and her feelings had to stay secret.

Lady Diana could hardly be expected to wear grand clothes when she spent almost every weekday working with lively little children. Instead jeans, casual cotton skirts, loose shirts, quilted jackets and woollen waistcoats were acceptable day to day wear. That way it didn't matter if her toddler charges daubed their sticky fingers over her clothes as they clutched her skirts or tugged at her sleeve. Today Diana still has a soft spot for children and she lets them run riot around her even when it means her designer-made silk or velvet clothes are in danger of getting a little dirty.

After months of speculation Lady Diana's engagement to the Prince of Wales was announced on February 24th 1981. A day or two earlier, Lady Diana realised she had no suitable clothes for the engagement picture which would follow the announcement. So she turned to her mother, the Hon. Mrs Shand Kydd and together they dashed to Harrods to buy a British-designed blue silk suit by Cojana. When the bride to be appeared on the steps of Buckingham Palace for the photographers that day she had taken off the Sloane Ranger style gold 'D' pendant she had worn so often in the past. But she still wore a man's large wrist watch – that was to be replaced later by a slim gold wristwatch from the Prince of Wales.

The engagement picture of Lady Diana and Prince Charles standing on the steps of Buckingham Palace tells an important chapter in the Princess' fashion story. Despite 19 years as a country girl and Sloane Ranger, Lady Diana could switch to grand formal style without any problems. Her aristocratic background helped – some maintain that looking Royal just means dressing like an aristocratic wedding guest. Lady Diana managed the first fashion hurdle with ease but she had not yet developed the panache which was to start a craze for 'Lady Di fashions'. That came with outside advice, trial and error and a lot of hard work.

From the moment Lady Diana's name was linked to that of Prince Charles, pictures of her appeared almost daily in newspapers and on TV. It was irksome and sometimes upsetting to have such constant press attention – Lady Diana's mother even wrote to The Times to complain about it. But at the same time it gave Lady Diana a chance to scrutinise herself and her clothes through objective eyes.

The first thing Lady Diana decided to do to lay the foundations of her Royal fashion career, was to lose weight. To many her size 12 measurements were a pleasure to look at – she certainly was not fat or even plump by any standards. But Lady Diana decided she had to slim. When her engagement was announced Lady Diana moved into her own apartment at Clarence House which meant that she could take her favourite form of exercise, swimming, in the Buckingham Palace pool every morning. In the afternoon she would sometimes don a leotard and work out in a dance class. The routine of exercise and sensible dieting whittled away at Lady Diana's curves, and soon she was down to a small size ten. Her rounded cheeks had vanished to reveal high cheekbones and an elfin, heartshaped face.

On the night of the engagement, while Londoners celebrated outside, the Prince of Wales took his bride to be to a quiet dinner at Clarence House with the Queen Mother and Ruth, Lady Fermoy who is the Queen Mother's old friend and Lady Diana's grandmother. In her youth the Queen Mother had almost as much influence on fashion as the Princess of Wales today. On a 1938 visit to Paris when the young Queen dressed in mourning white for her late mother, Norman Hartnell wrote: 'the Queen opened a parasol of transparent lace and tulle and delighted all the onlookers. At a stroke she resuscitated the art of the parasol makers of Paris and London'. During the War the Queen Mother firmly refused to wear a uniform while touring bomb sites and hospitals, "Why should one be drab?" she asked and continued to wear floaty pastel silks.

The Queen Mother's wafty pastel dresses, the little trains and pretty colour combinations weren't suitable for Lady Diana's age group. But, like the Queen Mother, she loves romantic clothes such as the charming lacy blouses which became a mainstay during the engagement.

It would not have gone completely amiss if Lady Diana had decided to break a royal tradition by going bare-headed for all but the most formal engagements and for events such as Ascot – after all Lady Diana was only 19 when she carried out her first engagements and few women wear hats today. But Lady Diana decided to go in for hats . . . in a big way. She turned to the Scottish born hatter John Boyd who already made hats for Princess Anne. Lady Diana's hats were a hit – and how!

One ostrich farmer in South Africa wrote to John Boyd, tongue in cheek, complaining that he could no longer supply the world demand for ostrich feathers – was it true that demand had rocketed because a young lady called Diana had started to wear ostrich feathers in her hats? Suddenly hats were back in fashion although few women could master the technique of wearing them as well as Lady Diana. According to the British Hat Guild many women were buying hats on the spur of the moment and storing them away without having the courage to wear them.

Lady Diana had no such qualms and paraded pill boxes, boaters, jaunty Robin Hood hats, sophisticated wider brimmed hats, straw hats, silk hats and veiled hats.

Lady Diana had plenty of original ideas about fashion – but she had to mould them to suit her role as the world's leading Princess and the wife of the heir to the British throne. For the couple's first formal evening together at Goldsmith's Hall Lady Diana wore a revealing black strapless ball dress designed by the Emanuel's, the couple destined to design her wedding dress. The effect was dramatic and breathtaking. What a contrast a few weeks later when Lady Diana wore a demure blue sailor suit and a string of pearls for a picture with the Prince of Wales and the Queen after the Privy Council had approved the marriage.

Choosing clothes for her new life was not easy – the Hon. Mrs Shand Kydd who had helped her daughter through the worst of the pre-engagement publicity took Lady Diana on several shopping trips – but she could not give the detailed fashion advice needed for a young lady about to become a member of the Royal family. So Lady Diana turned for help to Vogue, whose experts guided her through the Royal fashion maze.

Within weeks the results began to show. Lady Diana already looked every inch a Royal but she had added one or two idiosyncratic touches to her wardrobe. There were frilly, lacy and flounced collars which Lady Diana matched to many of her first Royal engagement outfits – the green silk, blue-trim suit she wore to the late Lord Mountbatten's home, Broadlands, the red and white silk suit she wore to a Gloucestershire hospital and the pale apricot suit she wore to Lady's Day at Ascot. Then there was the multi-stranded pearl choker Lady Diana wore as often as possible, and to cap it all the 'Lady Di hairstyle'. It had been cut and styled by Kevin Shanley at Headlines hair and beauty salon just down the road from Lady Diana's bachelor girl flat. Just a touch of tinting, and a little careful snipping and setting, and Kevin created the cut which is still one of the Princess' most striking features, although it has grown much longer since Lady Diana's engagement days.

As euphoria about the engagement died down, speculation about The Dress grew – above all – who would be asked to make the wedding dress. Sure enough, in line with Lady Diana's romantic turn of mind, she asked the Emanuels to design the dress. The couple specialise in fairy-tale style dresses with frills, bows, tight bodices, fussy, lacy sleeves, flounced skirts, huge petticoats and all the enchanting prettiness which captivated Lady Diana's heart. Silk worms in Dorset were put on overtime to produce enough thread for the dress, and no sooner had the announcement of Emanuel's scoop been made than their Brook Street workshops came under seige from photographers and reporters from all over the world hoping to get a glimpse of, or the tiniest hint about, The Dress. The wedding dress became one of the country's best guarded secrets.

It was worth it. Early on the morning of Wednesday July 29th 1981 Lady Diana was made up, her hair was styled and she was dressed for her wedding. Her make up included a certain amount of green foundation to take down her naturally high colour, and to disguise any bridal blushes. Her dress – ivory silk and old lace embroidered with mother of pearl sequins and pearls was tight-waisted with a flounced crinoline skirt and a twenty five foot train. It was the stuff that dreams are made of. Her veil, sparkling with sequins, was held in place by the Spencer family diamond tiara. With a deep breath Lady Diana set off for her carriage, and the journey to her new life.

The young bride walked into St Paul's, paused for a moment while the worst creases in her dress were smoothed, and then walked gracefully down the aisle on the arm of her father Earl Spencer. Every Head of State, every VIP, every guest in St Paul's that day fell silent and turned to watch Lady Diana in awe. There were critics who later said the dress didn't quite work – that it was too fussy, it looked too crumpled and that the colour did nothing for Lady Diana's complexion.

But for those of us inside the Cathedral on that sunny morning Lady Diana looked beautiful . . . every inch a fairy tale princess.

Back at the wildly happy reception at Buckingham Palace the Princess of Wales' sister Lady Sarah removed the Spencer family pearl choker she had been wearing so that the new Princess could wear it with her going away outfit. Both the Spencer sisters, Mrs Shand Kydd, and the ladies of the Royal family operate a jewel pool.

After a few days at Broadlands, the late Lord Mountbatten's home, the Royal couple boarded the Royal Yacht *Britannia* to complete their honeymoon with a tour of the Mediterranean. Once again the Princess of Wales demonstrated the wide variety of fashion she could wear. As they waved goodbye to Gibraltar the Princess was wearing a white silk dress decorated with flower sprigs. Later she was pictured on deck in a pith helmet style hat, a white shirt and bermuda shorts. By the time the honeymoon was over and the couple had flown to Balmoral the Princess posed for photographers in a country style brown tweed suit.

As the weather grew colder that winter we got used to seeing the Princess wearing coats for her engagements – coat dresses, Cossack-style coats with matching muff and hat, embroidered coats, multi-coloured wool coats and even furs. Soon her clothes had to be tailored to meet a new need – for the Princess of Wales was expecting her first baby. By the spring the Princess had discovered a pretty, comfortable dress design which suited her. So she had the waistless, yoked dress made up in several different fabrics and the design became the mainstay of her maternity wardrobe. Off duty the Princess maintained her relaxed, informal approach to dressing and at one polo match she even appeared in jeans and a jolly Koala motif jumper which stretched over her tummy. Tights were too irksome and hot to wear by the summer and instead the Princess took to wearing pop sox – they looked just like tights but they reached only to her knees.

Soon after William arrived the Prince and Princess went to Balmoral for the annual Royal holiday. By the time the holiday was over the Princess was quite naturally longing to get back into all the stunning clothes she had worn before she was pregnant – and to buy some new season clothes. She had hardly set foot in London before she did the round of so-called Tiara Triangle – some of the world's grandest shops including Harrods and Harvey Nichols and various top designer showrooms which make a triangle just down the road from the Princess' new home, Kensington Palace.

DIANA THE RADIANT PRINCESS

The Princess wasn't only buying for her hectic round of Royal engagements – she had to start planning her wardrobe for the coming tour of Australia and New Zealand. Only by scrutinising the fashions on offer could the Princess decide on what to have made for her six week tour down under. Her tall, leggy figure means she can wear just about anything, so her task was to decide on appropriate clothes for every engagement and for three climates – high summer in the desert, cooler summer in Victoria and autumn in New Zealand. So began months of visits from Vogue, of ordering dress samples at Kensington Palace, adding finishing touches to dresses and suits during fittings and finally ordering hats to go with all the outfits. Once again the Princess' dress secrets were well kept – not one designer spilled the beans before or even during the Princess' first tour.

But the clothes spoke for themselves. The Princess had found her own formula – her clothes made her look Royal, cheerful, pretty and fashionable all at once.
Alice Springs, the Prince and Princess' first stop shimmered in nearly 100 degrees – but the Jan Vanvelden dress in blue green silk that the Princess wore that day kept her looking cool. Every day on tour cameras clicked furiously to record the Princess' every move and every new outfit. Many of the hats, dresses, suits and coats were new – but some had been seen before in Britain. "Old" or new clothes; the press and public down under couldn't get enough of the Princess, and she drew crowds in their thousands. The Queen was so delighted with the couple's success she sent messages of congratulations.

On the last night of the Australian leg of the tour the Princess of Wales showed off a new dazzling Royal fashion departure – a body-hugging white silk evening dress embroidered with thousands of crystal beads. The one-shouldered dress was glamorous and sexy and it was the last thing anyone had expected the Princess of Wales to wear that night. There was another pleasant surprise when the Princess waved goodbye to Australia, for she was wearing a jokey, digger-style blue hat as a tribute to her hosts of the past month.

New Zealand was colder than had been expected and so coats became regular wear for the Princess. In Australia too the weather had been so cool and the Princess had worn many of the outfits originally designed for cool-weather New Zealand. So messages were sent to some of the Princess' designers and her hatter that she needed nine more cool-weather outfits to be made and flown out to her.

By the end of the New Zealand leg of the tour the Princess had conquered the Antipodes with smiles and style, and despite some out-of-touch Australian writers who complained her dresses were too long and told her, "Show us a leg Doy-an-ah" most agreed the Princess' fashions had hit just the right note. Her clothes had pleased fashion experts and court fogies alike. There was only one thing which had upset the Princess over her clothes on tour and before – the suggestion that she spent £1,500 a week on her wardrobe. Buckingham Palace will not give an exact figure but the Princess' Press Secretary Vic Chapman described the figure of £1,500 as "Ridiculous". As if to prove the point the Princess wore many old dresses and suits for her tour of Canada in June 1983.

After two years of Royal engagements and two major tours the Princess' simple silk, cotton or wool waisted suits and dresses matched with a jaunty-angled hat have become her staple day time working clothes. Those clothes are probably the best thing to have happened to the British fashion industry since Mary Quant and Jean Shrimpton.

But in the end the Princess, like the Queen Mother, is such a charming and attractive woman that she could probably make sack cloth look appealing.

Frilled, Chinese, crossover and wing collars –
the Princess of Wales' neck lines are often
the details which give an otherwise ordinary
dress chic. Not that the crowds bothered too
much about such minutiae – they just loved
Diana. 'She's GORGEOUS' was the cry
Down Under, and in Canada, 'Those lovely
eyes.'

You could say fashion went straight to the Princess of Wales' head – her hats, all designed by John Boyd of Knightsbridge – set a new craze for headwear. And that despite the fact that the Princess of Wales sometimes wears her hats the wrong way round – back to front or even sideways; the hats often look better for it. The Princess' first major hat event came at her first Ascot – and she passed with flying colours in a veiled pill box, a red boater and an ostrich feather hat. The Prince of Wales likes to see the Princess wearing hats with little veils which only just cover her eyes. The misty effect they give certainly highlights the Princess' stunning, wide blue eyes. One glance from them can make strong men crumble!

It didn't seem possible that the blushing young Sloane Ranger could transform her ultra-relaxed Sloane style – a mix of pin-striped skirts, lacy tops, baggy cotton print skirts, loose shirts and oversized pullovers – to a fashionable Royal elegance in two short years. But the Princess took her new job seriously, worked hard at her model girl looks and chose clothes which put her at the centre of the fashion world. Exercise and diet changed the Princess from a pretty young bachelor girl to a beautiful young woman. On tour she took her hairdresser, but no make up artist – nature gave the Princess all she needs.

Now and then the Princess abandoned demure pastel or primary colour blocks, pretty prints and discreet flower patterns in favour of stripes. Bold stripes, broad stripes . . . beautiful stripes. In Ottawa when the Princess wore the silk striped dress (above) she had already captured the heart of a man who knows more than enough about beautiful women – Canada's leader Pierre Trudeau, pictured behind the Princess. But for an Australian Church service two months earlier the Princess of Wales' stripes (left) were less flamboyant.

Touring with the Princess of Wales is like touring with a flower shop. No sooner does her official car stop than children rush forward to press posies into her arms. Every bunch, from large bunches of bought flowers, to tired-looking wild flowers little children pick in the countryside, are passed by the Princess to her Lady in Waiting or to policewomen. No sooner has the Princess accepted a few bunches and passed them back than more flowers are being presented, and sometimes even thrown by the excited crowds. As long as the flower givers put their names and addresses on their gift – no matter how small – they get a letter of thanks from the Princess' household.

Tiaras, said some, would be a problem – how could the Princess possibly wear a tiara with her 1980s hair style? Hairdresser Kevin Shanley proved it was no problem. As the pictures show, the Spencer Family tiara and the Queen Mary tiara look as if they were made for the Princess.

Come rain or shine the Princess had to look her best on tour and trunks were packed with everything from skimpy silk dresses to thick coats. On Ayers Rock the Princess wore a simple, crisp cotton dress by Benny Ong. It looked enviably cool but on the way down Ayers Rock it blew open revealing a slim Royal knee. The photographers below were delighted – the Princess wasn't so happy.

The eyes have it. In Australia many were worried that the meeting between the Royal couple and the newly-elected Republican leader Bob Hawke would be an awkward one. But the meeting went well, and when the Royals left Bob Hawke could only agree wholeheartedly with his wife that the Princess has beautiful eyes.

The red dress pictured here was originally made for the Princess to wear at Ascot – two years later the Princess wore it on tour in Australia.

If mum could do it so could the young Prince William! And on two of his earliest press calls the baby Prince showed that his wardrobe was as stylish as the Princess of Wales'. On the journey from his home from home in Australia, the sheep station Woomargama in New South Wales, to Melbourne, William sported the blue and white romper.

Clutching a Canadian flag, the Princess of Wales stayed loyal to British designers. Jasper Conran, Caroline Charles and Donald Campbell are among her favourites. But it will be another year before the Princess of Wales starts giving out her Royal warrants – and until then Buckingham Palace refuse to give out any information about her designers.

The black and white skirt and top by Jan Vanvelden was dubbed 'Di's disco number' when she gave it its first airing at an Adelaide student dance. It came as a surprise to see the Princess in the same clothes at the Governor General's sedate garden party in New Zealand.

Red and white was, appropriately, a colour theme for the Princess in Canada. The white hat trimmed with red (pictured here) went with two red and white outfits. Pillar box red suits the Princess and she wears it often in the day and during the evening. But most colours from pastel shades, through startling primary colours to black look good on the Princess. Orange is one of the few colours she does not wear.

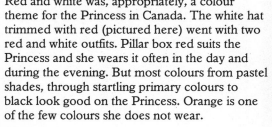

A hint of leg silhouetted through Jasper Conran's demure grey and white silk suit must have delighted the Prince of Wales. He loved the photograph of Lady Diana standing against the sun in a filmy skirt, taken while she was working at the Young England Kindergarten.

Looking Royal on every occasion is no easy task, so the Princess of Wales opts for natural fabrics – like cotton, wool and silk. Her off duty clothes are also natural fibre. The Princess loves unusual knitwear – her Sally Muir black sheep jumper is a favourite.

By day the Princess' fashions sparkle – by night they dazzle. The evening dresses and ballgowns she brought on tour showed how far the Princess' fashion sense had come since the pre-engagement days when her evening dresses were sometimes too revealing. In Sydney at the Wentworth Ball, Australian women had spent small fortunes in an effort to look their best, and arrived in everything from glittering space-age style evening wear to Victorian crinoline ball dresses. But that night, like every night on tour, the Princess' dress – she wore the blue and silver ruffled, by Bruce Oldfield – stole the show.

George VI gave aquamarines to the Queen Mother 'to match the sparkle of her eyes'. Today history seems to be repeating itself – the Princess of Wales has been showered with sapphires – the first was her diamond and sapphire engagement ring.

Remember that chic white suit the Princess of Wales wore in Tasmania? Here it is again but with a huge clown collar to give it a completely new look in New Brunswick, Canada. Canada or Down Under the suit was a hit – especially that coy little slit in the skirt.

Hats are fun as the Princess of Wales has shown, but she decided to go hatless on the last minute, informal tour of Victoria's bush fire area. Earlier on Ayers Rock, when she went bare headed in the blazing heat, some Aussies said she would have been better off with a hat.

In bustle, bows, lace and frills the Princess of Wales looked delightful – and her Klondike-style costume was set off by the prettiest pair of peach kid lace up boots ever seen in Edmonton, Canada. Later the Princess confessed her boned bodice was rather uncomfortable.

Hachi is the proud designer of a dress which took the fashion world by storm. His slinky, one-shouldered silk evening creation embroidered with crystal beads showed the Princess at her most glamorous. The designer, who has a workshop just off Bond Street, does not like traditional ball dresses – he likes his dresses to show a woman's body to its best advantage.

Everywhere the Princess went on tour she brought happiness and laughter with her. In blistering heat, in cold and in rain the Princess kept smiling.

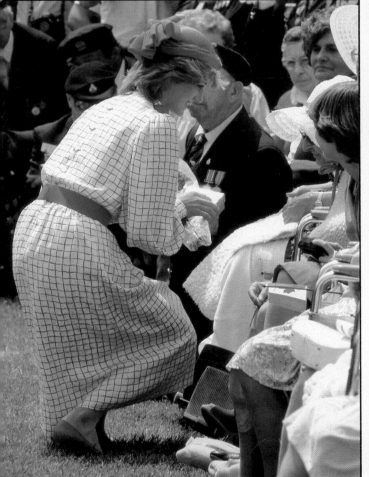

The Princess' designer wardrobe never stopped her doing the things which might dirty a dress or stain a skirt. If she spotted disabled or old people, or tiny children in the crowd, she would make a bee-line for them and crouch down to talk to them so they could hear her more easily. On tour in Canada when the Princess was given some flowers by a blind boy, she guided his hands over her face and clothes so he could feel the different textures.

Quilted jackets became an all important stand-by for the Princess of Wales in Australia and New Zealand, where the weather was very unpredictable. The floral jacket pictured is part of a suit designed by Miss Antonette. The Princess of Wales bought it off the peg from Harrods in the summer of 1982. Apart from wearing the suit in Melbourne she wore the jacket in New South Wales over the blue-green silk dress first worn at Alice Springs at the start of the tour. When the Princess wore the yellow quilted jacket pictured (above) in Waitangi, New Zealand, she managed to keep it crisp and neat despite the fact that the vast tribal canoe which carried her to Waitangi sprang a small leak just before she boarded.

It was their last evening in Canada, and the night before the Princess' birthday – and in celebration the Princess wore a dazzling new red evening dress to a small farewell dinner. Later she got her first official birthday present – a dressing table set in a deep red box decorated with a large red velvet bow.

Critics said the Princess' dresses were dowdy, middle-aged and, above all, too long. Few could agree with the first two criticisms. As for the latter, there is a practical reason for the Princess of Wales' longer than average dresses. She tends to bend over to talk with children and with people in wheelchairs, or to pick up cards and flowers thrown by eager admirers. By keeping her skirts longer rather than shorter the Princess has found she can avoid embarrassment.

One of the first pieces of jewellery the Princess of Wales made popular was the pearl choker. In the Spencer family jewel collection there is at least one fine, multi-string choker. Now the Princess can boast several pearl chokers in her own jewel collection.

Some of the Princess' fashion consciousness seemed to have worn off on the Prince by the time their first tour came round. Her hairdresser Kevin Shanley got to work on the Prince's hairstyle and swapped his old greased-down style for a bouncy, less formal cut which covered his bald patch and disguised his larger than average ears.

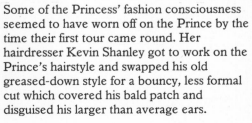

'Working the crowds' was second nature to the Princess of Wales by the time she had spent four weeks touring Australia. In New Zealand she even learned not to blush when admirers asked to kiss her hand or cheek.

Every now and then the Princess shows a romantic choice of colours similar to that of the Queen Mother. The Chelsea Design Company's pink and white fine striped dress is typical – it is just the kind of pastel pink the Queen Mother loves to wear.

At 22 years old the Princess of Wales has managed to acquire the easy confidence of an old campaigner. Her success in the fashion field helped build up that confidence, and the Princess' Royal fashion formula – traditional British frocks with a touch of Di magic like a special neckline, an unusual belt, strikingly bold colour combinations or out-of-the-ordinary cuffs – has been a much needed shot in the arm for the British fashion industry.